HANUMAN CHALISA

FOR KIDS & BEGINNERS

With word by word meaning and illustrations for easy understanding

This book belongs to :

· ·

 1 

Contents

Dedication

This book is dedicated to our Super Hero Hanuman, to my daughter Saanvi and to my husband Sriram.

Who is Hanuman?

Hanuman, which refers to a Vanara, is characterized by having a broad, prominent, or deformed jaw. In the Hindi-speaking region of India, the name signifies "one without ego, pride, and inflated self-image" (Maan).

When Hamuna was a child, he mistakenly thought the sun was a mango and flew into the sky in search of the fruit. He was struck by a thunderbolt known as a vajra of Lord Indra, which disfigured his jaw. Since "Hanu" means jaw and "man" means deformed in Sanskrit, Hanuman is a name given to him with affection. Each God granted Hanumanji a request as a result of Lord Indra's mistake: Lord Indra, may his body be as powerful as Indra's vajra. Fire won't harm him, says Lord Agni. Lord Varuna: He won't be harmed by water. Lord Vayu: He'll move as fast as the wind. Lord Brahma is able to travel everywhere. Lord Vishnu: "Gada" weapon. By combining these, Hanuman became an immortal with special abilities.

What is the Hanuman Chalisa ?

In the 16th century, Sage Tulsidas wrote the Awadhi version of the Hanuman Chalisa. (more than 400 years ago). Hanuman is one of the well-known characters in the Hindu epic "Ramayana" and a follower of Lord Rama. The monkey god Hanuman is the first superhero in Hindu mythology before there were Batman, Superman there was Hanuman

As it emphasizes Hanuman's distinct attributes, the Hanuman Chalisa has a specific place and significance in Hinduism. There are forty verses honouring Hanuman, and Soujanya Pasumarthi has translated each one so that kids can understand it.

Hanuman ji's qualities and miraculous power have been described and praised in forty verses in Hanuman Chalisa.

The meaning of the word Chalisa is forty (40), as this hymn has 40 verses or quatrains, excluding 2 couplets, hence this prayer is called Hanuman Chalisa. It is a popular prayer offered by devotees to please Lord Hanuman.

The Hanuman Chalisa is chanted to generate good vibrations and energy. Children that repeat the Hanuman Chalisa will possess power and wisdom. Children may attempt tasks that may be difficult or hard and may result in sadness or frustration. Children can overcome challenging difficulties by praying to Hanuman. He/she can achieve their well-being by bringing them inner serenity and joys.

Method of Hanuman Chalisa

For daily worship of Shri Ram devotee Hanumanji, the devotee should wear pure clothes (red as possible) and sit facing east or north and keep the idol or picture of Shri Hanuman ji in front of him. Red flowers, akshat, vermilion are used in worship material. Boondi, roasted gram and chironji seeds and coconut can be taken as Prasad. Devotees meditate on Shri Ram devotee Hanumanji by taking akshat and flower in their hand from the following shloka.

अतुलितबलधामं हेमशैलाभदेह, दनुजवनकृशानुं ज्ञानिनामागगण्यम्।
सकलगुणनिधाने वानराणामधीश, रघुपति प्रियभक्तवातजातं नमामी।।
मनोजवं मारुततुल्यवेगं जितेन्द्रियं बुद्धिमतां वरिष्ठम् ।
वातात्मजं वानरयूथमुख्यं श्रीरामदूतं शरणं प्रपद्ये ।।

Atulitbaldham Hemshailabhadeh, Danujavankrishanum Gyaninaamgraganyam.
Sakalgunnidhane Vanranamdhish, Raghupati Priyabhaktwatjaat Namami.
Manojvam Maruttulyvagam Jitendriyam Buddhimatam Seniorim.
Vaatatmajan Vanarayuthamukhyam Shri Ramdoot Sharanam Prapadye.

After this, start reciting Hanuman Chalisa by offering flowers, Akshat etc. After recitation, chant Om Hanu Hanu Hanu Hanumate Namah mantra 108 times.

Hanuman Chalisa can also be read during the journey. You can recite Hanuman Chalisa even at night. You can recite Hanuman Chalisa daily after taking bath in the morning. While reciting Hanuman Chalisa, sit on a red aasan and light a lamp of cow's ghee.

श्रीगुरु चरन सरोज रज निज मनु मुकुरु सुधारि ।
बरनउँ रघुबर बिमल जसु जो दायकु फल चारि ॥

Shreeguru charana saroja raja nija mana mukura sudhaari
baranau raghubara bimala jasu jo daayak phala chaari

"Cleaning my mind's mirror with the dust from Divine Guru's lotus feet, I now proceed to describe the spotless magnificence of Lord Rama.", which bestows four fruits of Righteousness (Dharma), Wealth (Artha), Pleasure (Kama) and Liberation (Moksha) "

[ShreeGuru=*revered Guruor teacher* ;Charana=*feet*; Saroja=*lotus*; Raja=*dust/ particle*; Nija=*Mine*;mana=*mind*;mukura=*mirror*; sudhaari=*Cleansing/applying*; Baranau=*Describe*; Raghubara=*Of Raghu Vamsha, Lord Rama*; Mala=*impurity*, Bimala=*pure*; Jasu=*Glory*; Jo=*which*, Daayak=*bestower*, Phala=*fruit*, Chaar=*four*]

बुद्धिहीन तनु जानिके, सुमिरौं पवन कुमार ।
बल बुधि विद्या देहु मोहि, हरहु कलेश विकार ॥

Buddhiheena tanu jaanikai sumirau pavanakumāra
Bal buddhi vidyā dehu mohi harahu kalesa vikāra

"Considering this person as less intelligence , I remember Lord Hanuman. O Hanuman the son of Vayu ; Give me strength, intelligence, and knowledge, cure my body ailments and mental imperfections"

[BuddhiHeena=*without intelligence*; tanu=*body, person*; jaanikai=*knowing*; sumirau=*remember*; pavanakumar=*son of wind god, Hanuman*; Bal=*strength*; Buddhi=*intelligence*; Vidya=*knowledge*; dehu=*give*; harahu=*remove, clear*; kalesa=*ailments*; vikara=*imperfections*]

जय हनुमान ज्ञान गुन सागर
जय कपीस तिहुँ लोक उजागर॥१॥

Jaya hanumāna Jnaana guna saagara
Jaya kapeesha tihu loka ujaagara

" Victory to Hanuman, who is the ocean of wisdom and virtue, and
the Monkey King, who is illuminating three worlds, "

[Jaya=*victory/ glory*; Jnaana=*Wisdom*; guna=*virtues/ qualities*; saagara=*ocean*;
Kapeesha=*King of Monkeys=Hanuman*; tihu=*three*; loka=*world*;
ujaagara=*illuminator*]

राम दूत अतुलित बल धामा
अंजनि पुत्र पवनसुत नामा॥२॥

**Rāma dūta atulita bala dhāmā
Anjani putra pavanasuta nāmā**

"You are the abode of unmatched power, and you are the messenger of Rama (to Sita)." You are also known as "Anjani Putra," which means "Son of Anjana," and "Pavana suta," which means "Son of the Wind God."

[Doota=*messenger*; *tulita*=*measured*; *atilita*=*immeasurable*; bala=*power*; dhama=*abode*; Anjani=*of Anjana*; putra=*son*; pavana=*wind*; suta=*son*; naama=*name*]

महाबीर बिक्रम बजरंगी
कुमति निवार सुमति के संगी॥३॥

Mahābīra bikrama bajarangī|
kumati nivāra sumati ke sangī

You are the bravest and greatest hero, mighty Hanuman, with a body as powerful as Indra's thunderbolt's weapon, the Vajrayudha. You are the destroyer of negative qualities and the friend of those with a pure (good) mind, as well as positive qualities and thoughts, so heal my bad mind.."

[Maha=*great*;Beera=*Brave*; Vikram=*great deeds*; bajra=*diamond*; ang=*body parts*; kumati=*bad intellect*; nivara=*cure, clean, destroy*; sumati=*good intelligence*; ke=*of*; sangi=*companion*]

कंचन बरन बिराज सुबेसा
कानन कुंडल कुँचित केसा॥४॥

**Kaanchana barana birāja subesā
kānana kundala kunchita keshā**

**"You have a golden complexion and shine in your beautiful attire.
You wear round earrings and have a beautiful curly hair."**

[Kaanchana=*golden*; barana=*hue*; birāja=*resplendent, shining*; subesā=*good attire/
good looks*; kānana=*ear*; Kundala=*ear-rings*; kunchita=*curly*; Kesha=*hair*]

हाथ बज्र अरू ध्वजा बिराजे
काँधे मूँज जनेऊ साजे॥५॥

**Hātha bajra au dhvajā birājai
kāndhe mūnji janeū sājai**

"Vajrayudha (mace)in one hand and flag shining in your hand. Sacred thread made of Munja grass adorns your shoulder"

[Hath=*hand*, Bajra=*Mace as powerful as vajrayudha or diamond*; au=*and*; dhvaja=*flag*; biraji=*take place*; kaandhe=*on shoulders*; munji=*of munja grass*; janeoo=*upavita thread, sacred thread*; Sajai=*adorn*]

शंकर सुवन केसरी नंदन
तेज प्रताप महा जगवंदन॥६॥

Shankara suvana kesarī nandana
Teja pratāpa mahā jaga Vandana

" incarnation of Lord shiva, giver of joy to King Kesari and son of kesari. The world respects and admires your great majesty.

[Shankara=*Lord shiva*; Kesari=*King Kesari, father of Hanuman*; Nandana=*son. joy giver*; Teja=*shine, grandness*; Pratapa=*prowess*; Maha=*great*; jaga=*world*;Vandana=*worship*]

विद्यावान गुनी अति चातु
राम काज करिबे को आतुर॥७॥

Vidyāvāna gunī ati chātura |
Rāma kāja karibe ko ātura

"Oh one learned in all Vidyas, one full of virtues, Very clever. You are always eager to do work for Rama's "

[Vidyavan=one who has learned Vidyas; Guni=having gunas; ati=very; chatura=clever; Kaaja=task, work; Karibe=doing, do; ko=to; Aatura=eager]

प्रभु चरित्र सुनिबे को रसिया
राम लखन सीता मनबसिया॥८॥

Prabhu charitra sunibe ko rasiyā
rāma lakhana sītā mana basiyā

"You enjoy listening to Lord Rama's story;
Lord Rama, Lakshman and Sita reside in your heart"

[Prabhu=*lord*; Charitra=*story, history*; sunibe=*hear*;
ko=*to*; Rasiya=*joy*; Mana=*mind*; Basiya=*reside, stay*]

सूक्ष्म रूप धरि सियहि दिखावा
विकट रूप धरि लंक जरावा॥९॥

**Sūkshma rūpa dhari siyahi dikhāvā
vikata rūpa dhari lanka jarāvā**

**"Assuming the smallest form you saw (visited) Sita.
Assuming the gigantic form you burnt down the Lanka"**

[sookshma=*micro, minute*; roopa=*form, body*; dhari=*assuming,
taking*; siyahi=*Sita*; Dikhava=*saw*; vikata=*enormous*;
Lanka=*Sri Lanka*; Jaraava=*burned*]

भीम रूप धरि असुर सँहारे
रामचंद्र के काज सवाँरे॥१०॥

Bhīma rūpa dhari asura samhāre
rāmachandra ke kāja samvāre

"Assuming a terrible form you slayed demons.
You made Lord Rama's works easier"

[Bheema=*terrible*; roopa=*form*; Dhari=*assuming*; Asura=*demon*; samhar=*destroy*;
Ramachandra=*Rama of Chandra Vamsha*;
Kaja=*work*; Samvare=*manage, make it easy, carry out*]

लाय सजीवन लखन जियाए
श्री रघुबीर हरषि उर लाए॥११॥

Lāya sanjīvani lakhana jiyāe
shrī raghubīra harashi ura lāye

**"You brought Sanjeevini mountain to save
Lakshmana's Life. Lord Rama embraced you in joy"**

[laaya=brought; Sanjeevani=a herb that brings back the dead; Lakhan=Lakshman;
Jiyaye=saved; Raghubira=Brave one of Raghu Clan, Lord Rama; Harashi=with joy;
Ura=neck; Laye=gave, brought]

रघुपति कीन्ही बहुत बड़ाई
तुम मम प्रिय भरत-हि सम भाई॥१२॥

Raghupati kīnhī bahut badāī
tum mama priya bharata hi sama bhāī

"Lord Rama praised you very much saying
'You are dear to me like my brother Bharata'"

[Raghupati=*King of Raghu Clan*; Bahut=*very much*; Badaayi=*praised*; Tum=*you*;
mama=*my, mine*; priya=*dear*; Bharata=*brother of Rama*;
hi=*like*; sama=*equal*; Bhai=*brother*]

सहस बदन तुम्हरो जस गावै
अस कहि श्रीपति कंठ लगावै॥१३॥

sahasa badana tumharo jasa gāvai
asa kahi shrīpati kantha lagāvai

**"'May the thousand headed serpent Adishesha sing of your glory'
saying this Lord Rama embraced you"**

[Sahasa=*thousand*; badan=*body*; Tumharo=*your*; Jasa=*success, glory*; Gaavai=*sing*;
asa=*like this*; kahi=*saying*; shripati=*husband of Goddess shree or Lakshmi, Lord
Rama*; Kantha=*neck*; Lagavai=*embrace*]

जय हनुमान

सनकादिक ब्रह्मादि मुनीसा
नारद सारद सहित अहीसा॥१४॥

**Sanakādika brahmādi munīsā
nārada sārada sahita ahīsā**

**"Sanaka, Brahma and other Royal sages,
Narad, Saraswati and Adishesha"**

[Sanaka=*sage sanaka*, adika=*other more*; brahma=*Creator Brahma*; Aadi=*and others*; Muneesha=*Royal sages*; Narada=*Sage Narad*; Sharada=*Goddess saraswati*; Sahita=*including*; Aheeshaa=*Adishesha*]

जम कुबेर दिगपाल जहाँ ते
कवि कोविद कहि सके कहाँ ते॥१५॥

**Yama kubera dikpāla jahā te
kavi kobida kahi sakai kahā te**

"Yama(the Gof of death., Kubera(God of wealth , Dikpaalakas, poets and singers; they can not describe your greatness properly"

[Yama=God of Time/death; Kubera=God of treasures; Dikpaalas=Gods of 8 directions; Kavi=poet; Kovida=singer; Kahi=how; Kaha=say;]

तुम उपकार सुग्रीवहि कीन्हा
राम मिलाय राज पद दीन्हा॥१६॥

**Tuma upakāra sugrīvahi kīnhā
rāam milāya rājapada dīnhā**

"You helped Sugreeva. You made him friends with Rama.Rama helped Sugriva defeat Vaali and helped him to get back his kingdom"

[Tuma=you; Upakaara=help; Sugreeva=Monkey King Sugreeva; Kinha=did; Milaaya=made them meet, join; Rajapada=kingship; Dinha=gave]

तुम्हरो मंत्र बिभीषण माना
लंकेश्वर भये सब जग जाना॥१७॥

**Tumharo mantra vibhīshana mānā
lankeshvara bhae saba jaga jānā**

**"Vibheeshana accepted your Suggestion. He became the king
of Lanka because of your advice, whole world knows it"**

*[Tmharo=your; mantra=words; Vibheeshan=brother of Raavan who
fought on Rama's side; Maana=accepted; Lankeshvara=King of Lanka; Saba=all;
Jaga=world; Jaana=knows]*

जुग सहस्त्र जोजन पर भानू
लिल्यो ताहि मधुर फ़ल जानू॥१८॥

**Juga sahasra yojana para bhānū
līlyo tāhi madhura phala jānū**

**"You flew towards the sun who is thousands of years of
Yojanas away, thinking of him as a sweet fruit"**

[J=year; Sahasra=thousand; Yojana=distance of 10-15km, 8 mile is the most agreed
upon distance; para=away; Bhanu=sun; Madhura=sweet; Phala=fruit; Janu=knowing,
thinking]

प्रभु मुद्रिका मेलि मुख माही
जलधि लाँघि गए अचरज नाही॥१९॥

**Prabhu mudrikā meli mukha māhī
jaladhi lānghi gaye acharaja nāhī**

"Putting the ring of Rama in your mouth, you jumped and flew over Ocean to Lanka, there is no surprise in that"

[Prabhu=*Lord*; Mudrika=*ring*; meli=*in,over*; Mukha=*mouth*; Mahi=*keeping*; jaladhi=*Ocean*; Laanghi gaye=*jumped*; Acharaja=*surprise*; Naahi=*no*]

दुर्गम काज जगत के जेते
सुगम अनुग्रह तुम्हरे तेते॥२०॥

**Durgama kāja jagata ke jete
sugama anugraha tumhare tete**

**"All the difficult tasks in the world,
become easy if there is your grace"**

[Durgama=*difficult*; Kaja=*task*; Jagata=*word*; Ke=*of*; Jete=*how many*; Sugama=*easy*;
Anugraha=*grace*; Tumhare=*your*; tete=*if there is*]

राम दुआरे तुम रखवारे
होत ना आज्ञा बिनु पैसारे॥२१॥

**Rāma duāre tuma rakhavāre
hota na āgyā binu paisāre**

**"Your the doorkeeper of Rama's court. Without your
permission nobody can enter Rama's abode"**

[Duare=*door*;tuma=*you*;rakhavaare=*keeper*; hota=*have, having*; na=*without*;
agyaa=*permission*; binu=*nobody*; paisaare=*enter, come in*]

सब सुख लहैं तुम्हारी सरना
तुम रक्षक काहु को डरना॥२२॥

**Saba sukha lahai tumhārī saranā
tuma rakshaka kāhū ko daranā**

**"All happiness stay with those who take refuge
in you. You are the protector, why be afraid? "**

[saba=*all*; sukha=*happiness, pleasures*; Lahai=*stay*; tumhari=*in your*; sarana=*refuge*;
tuma=*you*; rakshaka=*protector*; kahoo ko=*why? or of whom*; darana=*be afraid*]

आपन तेज सम्हारो आपै
तीनों लोक हाँक तै कापै॥२३॥

**āpan tej samhāro āpai
tino lok hānka te kāpai**

**"You are the only one who can control your power
and energy . All three worlds tremble in fear"**

*[Aapan=your; Tej=power; Samharo=destroy, control;
Apai=you; Tino=three; lok=worlds; hanka=fear; kapai=shake]*

भूत पिशाच निकट नहि आवै
महावीर जब नाम सुनावै॥२४॥

Bhūta pishācha nikata nahi āvai
mahābīra jaba nāma sunāvai

"Evil Spirits and Ghosts don't come near when your name is heard O great Courageous oneor when one chants Hanuma's name"

[Bhoota=*Evil spirits*, Pishaacha=*ghost*; nikata=*close*; nahi=*don't*; avai=*come*; mahabira=*maha+bira=great+brave*; jaba=*when*; naama=*name*; sunavai=*heard*]

जय हनुमान !
जय हनुमान
जय हनुमान
जय हनुमान !

नासै रोग हरे सब पीरा
जपत नरितर हनुमत बीरा॥२५॥

Nāsai roga harai saba pīrā
japata nirantara hanumata bīrā

"Diseases will be ended, all pains will be gone, when a devotee continuously repeats Hanuman's name"

[**Naasai**=*end, destroy*; **Roga**=*disease*; **Harai**=*end, close*; **Saba**=*all*; **Peera**=*pains, diseases, afflictions*; **Japata**=*keep repeating, remembering*; **nirantara**=*continuously*; **Beera**=*Brave*]

संकट तै हनुमान छुडावै
मन क्रम वचन ध्यान जो लावै॥२६॥

**Sankata te hanumāna chhudāvai
mana krama vachana dhyāna jo lāvai**

" If someone prays to Hanuman with their words, actions, and thoughts, they will be freed from their problems. "

[Sankata=*troubles, difficulties*; te=*from*; Chhudaavai=*release*; mana=*mind*; krama=*actions*; vachana=*words*; dhyana=*meditate, contemplate*; jo=*who*; Lavai=*apply, do, bring*]

सब पर राम तपस्वी राजा
तिनके काज सकल तुम साजा॥२७॥

Saba para rāma tapasvī rājā
tina ke kāja sakala tuma sājā

"Rama is the king of all, he is the king of yogis. You managed all his tasks and fulfilled all the missions of Sri Rama" or in other translation "He whoever takes refuge in Rama you will fulfil the desire of devotees"

[Saba=*all*; para=*on*; Tapasvi=*one of austerities*; Raja=*king*; Tina ke=*whose*; Kaaja=*work*; tuma=*you*; saaja=*carried*]

राम
राम
राम

और मनोरथ जो कोई लावै
सोई अमित जीवन फल पावै॥२८॥

Aura manoratha jo koī lāvai
Soi amita jīvana phala pāvai

"Whoever brings many of their wishes to you, their wishes are fulfilled beyond any limits will get imperishable fruits of liberation"

[aur=*many, more*; Manoratha=*mental wishes, desires*;
jo koi=*whoever*; Lavai=*brings*; amita=*infinite*; jivana=*life*;
phala=*fruits*; pavai=*get, receive*]

चारों जुग परताप तुम्हारा
है परसिद्ध जगत उजियारा॥२९॥

chāro juga pratāpa tumhārā
hai parasiddha jagata ujiyārā

"Your glory is for all the four yugas, Your greatness is very famous throughout the world, and illumines the world"

[Charo=*four*; juga=*yugas*; pratapa=*glory*; tumhara=*your*; hai=*is*; prasiddha=*famous*; jagata=*world*; ujiyara=*illumined, spread*]

साधु संत के तुम रखवारे
असुर निकंदन राम दुलारे॥३०॥

**Sādhu santa ke tuma rakhavāre
asura nikandana rāma dulāre**

**"You are the guardian of Saints and Good people.
You killed demons and you are dear to Rama"**

[Sadhu=*good people, monks, simple people*; Santa=*saint*; ke=*of*;
tuma=*you*; Rakhavaare=*keeper, guardian*; Asura=*demons*; Nikandana=*slayer*;
Dulare=*dear*]

अष्ट सिद्धि नौ निधि के दाता
अस बर दीन जानकी माता॥३१॥

Ashta siddhi nava nidhi ke dātā
asa bara dīnha jānakī mātā

**"Mother Sita granted you a boon to become the bestower of
8 Siddhis (supernatural powers) and 9 Nidhis (divine treasures)"**

[Ashta=*eight*; Siddhi=*supernatural powers*; Nava=*nine*; Nidhi=*treasures*; Ke=*of*;
Daata=*giver*; Asa=*like that*; bara=*boon*; Dinha=*give or gave*; Janaaki=*daughter of
Janaka, Sita*; Maata=*mother*]

राम रसायन तुम्हरे पासा
सदा रहो रघुपति के दासा॥३२॥

Rāma rasāyana tumhare pāsā
sadā raho raghupati ke dāsā

"You have the sweet devotion to Rama. May you always be a devotee of Lord Rama"

[Ras=*devotion, sweetness, love;* Rasaayana=*mixture or collection of sweetness;* tumhaare=*your;* paasa=*near;* Sadaa=*always;* Raho= *stay;* Raghupati=*Lord of Raghu Clan, Lord Rama;* Ke=*of;* Daasa=*servant, devotee*]

तुम्हरे भजन राम को पावै
जनम जनम के दुख बिसरावै॥३३॥

**Tumhare bhajana rāma ko pāvai
Janama janama ke dukha bisarāvai**

**"Singing your name gets us Rama himself and
Removes the sufferings of many lives"**

[Tumhare=*your*; Bhajana=*chanting*; Ko=*to*; Pavai=*takes to,
gives*; Janama=*life*; Janama janama=*life after life*; Ke=*of*; dukha=*unhappiness*;
Bisaravai=*remove*]

राम

अंतकाल रघुवरपुर जाई
जहाँ जन्म हरिभक्त कहाई॥३४॥

**Anta kāla raghupati pura jāī
jahā janma hari bhakta kahāī**

"He who sings of you, at the end of the life he attains to Lord Rama's abode. Where he will be born as a Devotee of Lord Rama"

[Anta=*End*; Kaala=*time*; Raghupati=*Lord of Raghu clan, Rama*; pura=*city*; Jaaee=*go*; Jaha=*where*; janma=*born*; Hari= *Lord Rama*; Bhakta=*devotee*; Kahai=*called as, is said*]

और देवता चित्त ना धरई
हनुमत सेई सर्व सुख करई॥३५॥

**Aura devatā chitta na dharaī
hanumata sei sarva sukha karaī**

**"Not contemplating on other gods, gets his all
happiness from Hanuman by serving him"**

[Aura=more, other; Devata=gods; chitta=mind; na=dont; Dharai=contemplating;
Sei=serving; sarva=all; sukha=happiness]

संकट कटै मिटै सब पीरा
जो सुमिरै हनुमत बलबीरा॥३६॥

Sankata katai mitai saba pīrā
jo sumirai hanumata balabīrā

"Pains will be removed, all afflictions will be gone
of who remembers Hanuman the mighty brave one"

[Sankata=*trouble*; katai=*cut short*; Mitai=*removed*; Saba=*all*; Peera=*pains, troubles*;
Jo=*who*; Sumirai=*remembers*; Bala=*power*; Bira=*brave*]

जै जै जै हनुमान गुसाईँ
कृपा करहु गुरू देव की नाई॥३७॥

**Jaya jaya jaya hanumāna gosāī
kripā karahu gurudeva kī nāī**

**"Victory to you O master of the senses.
Show mercy on us like a Guru does"**

[Jaya=victory; Gosai=master of senses; kripaa=mercy,
compassion; karahu=do, show; guru=teacher, dispeller of
darkness; Deva=god; Ki nai=like;]

जो सत बार पाठ कर कोई
छूटहि बंदि महा सुख होई॥३८॥

**Jo shata bāra pāthakar koī
chhūtahi bandi mahāsukha hoī**

**"He whoever recits this hundred times, his chains of
Bondage will be cut, Great happiness will be his"**

[Jo=*whoever*; Shata=*hundred*; Baar=*times*; Paathakar=*reciting*; chhutahi=*cut,
removed*; bandi=*shackles, bondage*; Mahasukha=*great happiness, bliss*; Hoi=*happens,
gets to*]

जो यह पढ़े हनुमान चालीसा
होय सिद्ध साखी गौरीसा॥३९॥

**Jo yaha padhai hanumāna chālīsā
hoya siddhi sākhī gaurīsā**

"He whoever reads these verses on Hanuman, he will get spiritual attainments, Lord Shiva is the witness to this statement, he will enjoy great happiness"

[Jo=who; yaha=this; Padhai=reads; Chalisa=40 lined hymn; Hoya=happens; Siddhi=attainments; Saakhi=witness; Gaureesha=Gowri+isha=Husband of Gowri=Lord Shiva;]

hanuman
chalisa

तुलसीदास सदा हरि चेरा
कीजै नाथ हृदय मह डेरा॥४०॥

Tulasīdāsa sadā hari cherā
kījai nātha hridaya mama dherā

"Tulasidas is always a disciple of Lord Rama. O lord make my heart your abode(your home), please reside in my heart"

[Sada=*always*; Hari= *Lord Vishnu=Lord Rama*; Chera=*disciple, devotee*; Kijai=*please do*; Natha=*Lord*; Hridaya=*heart*; mama=*my, mine*; Dheraa=*abode*]

पवन तनय संकट हरन, मंगल मूरति रूप।
राम लखन सीता सहित, हृदय बसहु सुर भूप॥

pavanatanaya sankata harana mangala mūrati rūpa
rāma lakhana sītā sahita hridaya basahu sura bhūpa

**"O Son of wind god, remover of difficulties, oh one of auspicious form.
With Ram, Lakshman and Sita reside in our hearts of King of Gods"**

[Pavanatanaya=Pavana+tanaya=Wind+son, son of wind god, Hanuman;
Sankata=trouble; Harana=remover; Mangala=auspicious; Murati=statue, form;
Rupa=form; Sahita=including; Hridaya=heart; Basahu=reside; Sura=gods;
Bhupa=king]

ACTIVITY - 1

Make Hanuman colorful

ACTIVITY - 2

Help Hanuman find
its way to the Sun

ACTIVITY - 3

Draw Hanuman easily!

ACTIVITY - 4

Find the words!

```
R  L  O  R  D  H  A  N  U  M  A  N  I  D  P  A  J  S
P  O  E  L  O  Q  U  E  N  T  W  R  N  E  U  N  L  T
A  H  E  A  L  T  H  T  Q  I  R  E  T  V  D  J  O  R
V  K  B  U  T  U  L  S  I  D  A  S  E  O  I  A  R  E
A  E  J  D  S  I  T  A  M  A  A  J  L  T  V  N  D  N
N  S  H  A  N  U  M  A  N  C  H  A  L  I  S  A  R  G
P  H  B  D  A  T  C  R  B  N  A  P  I  O  G  T  A  T
U  A  H  D  Z  W  B  I  F  D  X  Q  G  N  B  M  M  H
T  R  I  C  O  U  R  A  G  E  Z  H  E  R  Q  Z  A  H
R  I  M  C  R  W  I  S  D  O  M  D  N  X  F  E  K  S
A  V  A  F  A  M  O  U  S  K  F  O  C  U  S  E  D  N
E  Q  F  E  A  R  L  E  S  S  S  Q  E  N  H  I  A  Q
```

ANJANA	FOCUSED	PAVAN PUTRA
BHIMA	HANUMAN CHALISA	SITA MAA
COURAGE	HEALTH	STRENGTH
DEVOTION	INTELLIGENCE	TULSIDAS
ELOQUENT	KESHARI	WISDOM
FAMOUS	LORD HANUMAN	
FEARLESS	LORD RAMA	

English Hanuman Chalisa

DOHA 1

Shreeguru charana saroja raja nija mana mukura sudhaari
baranau raghubara bimala jasu jo daayak phala chaari

DOHA 2

Buddhiheena tanu jaanikai sumirau pavanakumāra
Bal buddhi vidyā dehu mohi harahu kalesa vikāra

CHOUPAI

Jaya hanumāna Jnaana guna saagara
Jaya kapeesha tihu loka ujaagara

Rāma dūta atulita bala dhāmā
Anjani putra pavanasuta nāmā

Mahābīra bikrama bajarangī
kumati nivāra sumati ke sangī

Kaanchana barana birāja subesā
kānana kundala kunchita keshā

Hātha bajra au dhvajā birājai
kāndhe mūnji janeū sājai

Shankara suvana kesarī nandana
Teja pratāpa mahā jaga Vandana

Vidyāvāna gunī ati chāturā
Rāma kāja karibe ko ātura

Prabhu charitra sunibe ko rasiyā
rāma lakhana sītā mana basiyā

Sūkshma rūpa dhari siyahi dikhāvā
vikata rūpa dhari lanka jarāvā

Bhīma rūpa dhari asura samhāre
rāmachandra ke kāja samvāre

Lāya sanjīvani lakhana jiyāe
shrī raghubīra harashi ura lāye

Raghupati kīnhī bahut badāī
tum mama priya bharata hi sama bhāī

sahasa badana tumharo jasa gāvai
asa kahi shrīpati kantha lagāvai

Sanakādika brahmādi munīsā
nārada sārada sahita ahīsā

Yama kubera dikpāla jahā te
kavi kobida kahi sakai kahā te

Tuma upakāra sugrīvahi kīnhā
rāam milāya rājapada dīnhā

Tumharo mantra vibhīshana mānā
lankeshvara bhae saba jaga jānā

Juga sahasra yojana para bhānū
līlyo tāhi madhura phala jānū

Prabhu mudrikā meli mukha māhī
jaladhi lānghi gaye acharaja nāhī

Durgama kāja jagata ke jete
sugama anugraha tumhare tete

Rāma duāre tuma rakhavāre
hota na āgyā binu paisāre

Saba sukha lahai tumhārī saranā
tuma rakshaka kāhū ko daranā

āpan tej samhāro āpai
tino lok hānka te kāpai

Bhūta pishācha nikata nahi āvai
mahābīra jaba nāma sunāvai

Nāsai roga harai saba pīrā
japata nirantara hanumata bīrā

Sankata te hanumāna chhudāvai
mana krama vachana dhyāna jo lāvai

Saba para rāma tapasvī rājā
tina ke kāja sakala tuma sājā

Aura manoratha jo koī lāvai
Soi amita jīvana phala pāvai

chāro juga pratāpa tumhārā
hai parasiddha jagata ujiyārā

Sādhu santa ke tuma rakhavāre
asura nikandana rāma dulāre

Ashta siddhi nava nidhi ke dātā
asa bara dīnha jānakī mātā

Rāma rasāyana tumhare pāsā
sadā raho raghupati ke dāsā

Tumhare bhajana rāma ko pāvai
Janama janama ke dukha bisarāvai

Anta kāla raghupati pura jāī
jahā janma hari bhakta kahāī

Aura devatā chitta na dharaī
hanumata sei sarva sukha karaī

Sankata katai mitai saba pīrā
jo sumirai hanumata balabīrā

Jaya jaya jaya hanumāna gosāī
kripā karahu gurudeva kī nāī

Jo shata bāra pāthakar koī
chhūtahi bandi mahāsukha hoī

Jo yaha padhai hanumāna chālīsā
hoya siddhi sākhī gaurīsā

Tulasīdāsa sadā hari cherā
kījai nātha hridaya mama dherā

DOHA 3
pavanatanaya sankata harana mangala mūrati rūpa
rāma lakhana sītā sahita hridaya basahu sura bhūpa

Hindi Hanuman Chalisa

दोहा 1

श्रीगुरु चरन सरोज रज निज मनु मुकुरु सुधारि ।
बरनउँ रघुबर बिमल जसु जो दायकु फल चारि ॥

दोहा 2

बुद्धिहीन तनु जानिके, सुमिरौं पवन कुमार ।
बल बुधि विद्या देहु मोहि, हरहु कलेश विकार ॥

चौपाई

जय हनुमान ज्ञान गुन सागर
जय कपीस तिहुँ लोक उजागर॥१॥

राम दूत अतुलित बल धामा
अंजनि पुत्र पवनसुत नामा॥२॥

महाबीर बिक्रम बजरंगी
कुमति निवार सुमति के संगी॥३॥

कंचन बरन बिराज सुबेसा
कानन कुंडल कुँचति केसा॥४॥

हाथ बज्र अरू ध्वजा बिराजे
काँधे मूँज जनेउ साजे॥५॥

शंकर सुवन केसरी नंदन
तेज प्रताप महा जगवंदन॥६॥

विद्यावान गुनी अति चातु
राम काज करिबे को आतुर॥७॥

प्रभु चरित्र सुनिबे को रसिया
राम लखन सीता मनबसिया॥८॥

सूक्ष्म रूप धरि सियहि दिखावा
विकट रूप धरि लंक जरावा॥९॥

भीम रूप धरि असुर सँहारे
रामचंद्र के काज सवाँरे॥१०॥

लाय सजीवन लखन जियाए
श्री रघुबीर हरषि उर लाए॥११॥

रघुपति कीन्ही बहुत बड़ाई
तुम मम प्रिय भरत-हि सम भाई॥१२॥

सहस बदन तुम्हरो जस गावै
अस कहि श्रीपति कंठ लगावै॥१३॥

सनकादिक ब्रह्मादि मुनीसा
नारद सारद सहित अहीसा॥१४॥

जम कुबेर दिगपाल जहाँ ते
कवि कोविद कहि सके कहाँ ते॥१५॥

तुम उपकार सुग्रीवहि कीन्हा
राम मिलाय राज पद दीन्हा॥१६॥

तुम्हरो मंत्र बिभीषण माना
लंकेश्वर भये सब जग जाना॥१७॥

जुग सहस्त्र जोजन पर भानू
लिल्यो ताहि मधुर फ़ल जानू॥१८॥

प्रभु मुद्रिका मेलि मुख माही
जलधि लाँघि गए अचरज नाही॥१९॥

दुर्गम काज जगत के जेते
सुगम अनुग्रह तुम्हरे तेते॥२०॥

राम दुआरे तुम रखवारे
होत ना आज्ञा बिनु पैसारे॥२१॥

सब सुख लहैं तुम्हारी सरना
तुम रक्षक काहु को डरना॥२२॥

आपन तेज सम्हारो आपै
तीनों लोक हाँक तै कापै॥२३॥

भूत पिशाच निकट नहि आवै
महावीर जब नाम सुनावै॥२४॥

नासै रोग हरे सब पीरा
जपत निरंतर हनुमत बीरा॥२५॥

संकट तै हनुमान छुडावै
मन क्रम वचन ध्यान जो लावै॥२६॥

सब पर राम तपस्वी राजा
तिनके काज सकल तुम साजा॥२७॥

और मनोरथ जो कोई लावै
सोई अमित जीवन फल पावै॥२८॥

चारों जुग परताप तुम्हारा
है परसिद्ध जगत उजियारा॥२९॥

साधु संत के तुम रखवारे
असुर निकंदन राम दुलारे॥३०॥

अष्ट सिद्धि नौ निधि के दाता
अस बर दीन जानकी माता॥३१॥

राम रसायन तुम्हरे पासा
सदा रहो रघुपति के दासा॥३२॥

तुम्हरे भजन राम को पावै
जनम जनम के दुख बिसरावै॥३३॥

अंतकाल रघुवरपुर जाई
जहाँ जन्म हरिभक्त कहाई॥३४॥

और देवता चित्त ना धरई
हनुमत सेई सर्व सुख करई॥३५॥

संकट कटै मिटै सब पीरा
जो सुमिरै हनुमत बलबीरा॥३६॥

जै जै जै हनुमान गुसाईं
कृपा करहु गुरू देव की नाई॥३७॥

जो सत बार पाठ कर कोई
छूटहि बंदि महा सुख होई॥३८॥

जो यह पढ़े हनुमान चालीसा
होय सिद्ध साखी गौरीसा॥३९॥

तुलसीदास सदा हरि चेरा
कीजै नाथ हृदय मह डेरा॥४०॥

दोहा 3

पवन तनय संकट हरन, मंगल मूरति रूप।
राम लखन सीता सहित, हृदय बसहु सुर भूप॥

Author - About Soujanya Pasumarthi

A passionate Educationist. She is a Published author of Mumma, Papa, teach me a Shloka!, a book about story oriented shloka book . She founded Mystical Tale. It is leading storytelling (mythology, moral, STEM-based), shloka (Bala-siksha Holistic character building and child development program), public speaking, workshops for parents and kids and yoga academy for kids. Simplifies the learning experience. It is a platform for E-learning worldwide and a one-stop destination for all kid's needs. Passing on the timeless Indian traditions with scientific reasons for your children. Soujanya takes charge of introducing kids to their roots.

Illustrator - Priyanka Rani Dora

A self-taught illustrator residing in the vibrant city of Sambalpur, Odisha. With a passion for making things colorful, she enjoys the art of illustration, infusing life and joy into her creations. Her self-taught journey reflects her remarkable dedication and talent, creating captivating works of art. Her instagram art page will take you to another journey of art and colours named as doodlerdora .